D1712655

Biology

Understanding Living Matter

Biology

Understanding Living Matter

Edited by Melissa Landon

Britannica®
Educational Publishing

IN ASSOCIATION WITH

ROSEN
EDUCATIONAL SERVICES

Published in 2015 by Britannica Educational Publishing (a trademark of Encyclopædia Britannica, Inc.) in association with The Rosen Publishing Group, Inc.
29 East 21st Street, New York, NY 10010

Distributed exclusively by Rosen Publishing.
To see additional Britannica Educational Publishing titles, go to rosenpublishing.com.

First Edition

Britannica Educational Publishing
J.E. Luebering: Director, Core Reference Group
Anthony L. Green: Editor, Compton's by Britannica

Rosen Publishing
Hope Lourie Killcoyne: Executive Editor
Bethany Bryan: Editor
Intro and additional text by Diane Bailey
Nelson Sá: Art Director
Michael Moy: Designer
Cindy Reiman: Photography Manager
Marty Levick: Photo Researcher

Library of Congress Cataloging-in-Publication Data

Biology (Britannica Educational Publishing)
Biology: understanding living matter/edited by Melissa Landon.—First edition.
        pages cm.—(The study of science)
Audience: Grades 7 to 12.
Includes bibliographical references and index.
ISBN 978-1-62275-409-0 (library bound)
1. Biology—Juvenile literature. I. Landon, Melissa, editor. II. Title.
QH309.2.B554 2015
570—dc23
                                                                          2014007454

Manufactured in the United States of America

On the cover: © *iStockphoto.com/Andrey Prokhorov; cover and interior pages borders and backgrounds* © *iStockphoto.com/LuMaxArt*

CONTENTS

A male robin feeds an earthworm to his unfledged young. Scientists who study birds are known as ornithologists. Mike Truchon/Shutterstock.com

Life has existed on Earth for billions of years—always changing and adapting. New forms of life have evolved as old ones have become extinct. From the first, simplest organisms, Earth has given rise to millions of species. Some are familiar—the various kinds of plants and animals that we know—but many more are so tiny or so rare that they are known only to a handful of specialists.

Scientists who study living organisms are biologists. Within that broad definition are dozens of subspecialties. Some biologists study a certain category of life, while others focus on the patterns that connect all life-forms. Biologists look at the big picture—environments and organisms—as well as the tiny building blocks of cells and molecules.

Although there has been life on Earth for a long time, it was not always here. In its first billion years, Earth was a planet made up only of inanimate substances, such as minerals and gases. The mysteries surrounding how life first came to exist are some of the most fascinating in the field of biology. Equally fascinating are the questions concerning how life-forms have adapted—or failed to adapt—to their environments. Why are some plants carnivorous? Why did the dodo bird become extinct? Why are some bacteria deadly to humans but cause

no harm to other animals? Why do humans have blood, but trees have sap? How do some species survive in extreme temperatures? Life is not only infinitely variable but also incredibly tenacious. Although individual organisms within a species die, and even an entire species may become extinct (die out), life itself survives.

As recently as a few centuries ago, people had little idea how life initially began, nor did they understand exactly how it worked. They had neither the tools nor the vocabulary to accurately observe and describe the incredible complexity of living organisms. The tireless work of several influential scientists helped change that by offering explanations to how and why species change over time and by developing systems to categorize an eventual torrent of biological information.

The study of biology is vast, encompassing an understanding of what defines life and how life works and how it continues to change. The following pages examine the discipline of biology as a whole. They not only look at the fundamentals of biological processes and how species relate to each other and the environment but also explore the important discoveries that have influenced biology over the centuries and how the different disciplines within biology interact with each other.

As the body of knowledge grows, biologists can provide insights that help in other fields, such as medicine, anthropology, and even history. As environmental issues become more pressing, biology can inform the debate about how these problems arose and how to find solutions. Biologists have answered some of the questions of how life works, but many questions remain, and new ones constantly arise. Indeed, perhaps the most intriguing questions to consider are those that have not yet been asked.

CHAPTER 1

THE STUDY OF LIVING THINGS

The scientific study of living things is called biology. Biologists strive to understand the natural world and its living inhabitants—plants, animals, fungi, protozoa, algae, bacteria, archaea, and viruses—by asking why and how the processes of life occur. Why do living organisms interact with each other in particular ways? When did they evolve? How are biological processes carried out within organs, tissues, and cells? To answer these broad questions biologists must answer many specific ones: How does an animal's liver break down fat? How does a green plant convert water and carbon dioxide into sugar? Where do mosquitoes go in the winter?

Some investigations require years of scientific research. Today many mysteries remain unsolved, but continued study leads toward a better understanding of living things and the environment they depend on.

Rain forests like this one in Dominica are estimated to contain millions of different life-forms, many of which have not been discovered yet. Randolph Femmer/NBII Image Gallery

The annual output of biological research today is so massive that no single individual can possibly acquire all of the information. Because of this, areas of specialization have developed, allowing scientists to focus on their own research, yet remain informed on key developments in their fields.

SUBDIVISIONS OF BIOLOGY

The study of biology can be divided in various ways. Certain areas of research incorporate information from other sciences, such as physics, chemistry, or geology. For example, detailed studies of bioluminescence—the light produced by organisms such as fireflies—require a solid understanding of biochemistry.

Some biologists focus their research on one or several groups of organisms. Such specializations can be broad, such as zoology (the study of animals) and botany (the study of plants), or they can be specific, as in the following fields:

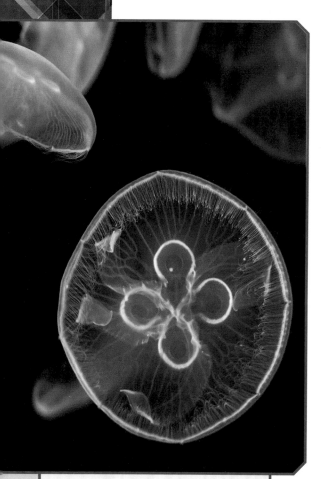

The moon jellyfish is bioluminescent, meaning it can produce its own light in the dark depths of the sea. Richard A McMillin/Shutterstock.com

BIOCHEMISTRY

Scientists in the field of biochemistry study the chemical basis of life's activities. They have shown that all living things—amoebas and elephants alike—share many similarities at the level of atoms and molecules. Without exception, all animals and plants operate on the basis of a few unvarying biological principles. These principles are: all forms of life consist of basic units called cells; every living thing has a heredity; all vital activities require energy; all cells undergo certain key chemical reactions; and all living groups reproduce.

Arachnology: spiders, mites, scorpions
Bryology: mosses
Entomology: insects
Herpetology: reptiles and amphibians
Ichthyology: fishes
Mammalogy: mammals
Microbiology: microscopic organisms
Mycology: fungi
Ornithology: birds
Parasitology: parasites
Phycology: algae
Virology: viruses

Some biologists study specific features, such as structure, or explore broad biological

The great blue heron was one of the many species described by Carolus Linnaeus, whose system of classifying organisms is used by all biologists. Gregory Johnston/Shutterstock.com

concepts. Such studies often look for general principles that apply to different types of organisms. Some examples are:

Anatomy: the structure of living things
Cytology: cells
Ethology: animal behavior
Genetics: heredity
Pathology: disease and its effect on the body
Physiology: biological functions

Primatologists study apes such as these mountain gorillas, which are part of the Nkuringo gorilla group at Bwindi Impenetrable National Park in Uganda. Photodynamic/Shutterstock.com

Biologists may be identified by the group of organisms they study or by their area of research. For example, a scientist who studies nonhuman primates (such as apes and monkeys) is called a primatologist; a scientist who studies genetics is called a geneticist.

The following sections discuss a small fraction of the many specialized areas of biological research.

CHAPTER 2

THE BRANCHES OF BIOLOGY

To understand the field of biology, it is often easiest to take a look at the individual branches within biology.

EMBRYOLOGY AND DEVELOPMENTAL BIOLOGY

Developmental biologists examine the processes that govern the growth and development of organisms. Included within the field are studies of embryological development of plants or animals and the natural phenomenon of regeneration in which removed cells, tissues, or entire structures of an organism grow back. Research in development has direct applications for agriculture and for human and veterinary medicine. An example of this is cloning, in which cells from an adult plant or animal are used to grow a genetically identical individual.

Stem cell researchers hope that their work will lead to new treatments for diseases such as Parkinson disease and diabetes. Spencer Platt/Getty Images

Plant cloning is widely used in agriculture and horticulture. Several types of animals, such as sheep, cows, and cats, have been cloned, though the practice is not widespread. Stem cell research is another example of developmental biology. The capability of stem cells (cells in very early stages of development) to grow many different kinds of living tissue in laboratory cultures has broad potential in medicine. Despite their potential in medicine, however, cloning and stem cell research remain controversial.

STEM CELL RESEARCH

There are hundreds of different types of cells in the human body. Most of them start out as stem cells. Stem cells contain the instructions needed to make the cell grow into a specialized type, such as a muscle, nerve, or blood cell. The ways that stem cells develop into specialized cells are not yet fully understood.

Scientists are working on the idea that a stem cell can be instructed to grow into a particular type of cell, such as a liver cell. If enough liver cells are grown to produce liver tissue that works normally, they could be transplanted into a person whose own liver has failed. This research could lead to treatments for many conditions and diseases, including Alzheimer disease, Parkinson disease, heart disease, diabetes, and damage to the spinal cord.

Some types of stem cells come from embryos (unborn babies that are still at a very early stage of development). Embryos are sometimes created in a laboratory as part of a process to help people have babies. Scientists can take cells called an egg from a woman and sperm from a man and combine them in the laboratory. The embryos that are created in this way can then be placed inside the woman's body to allow the baby to develop, or they can be kept in the laboratory. Some of the embryos are donated for use in research. Scientists can also get embryonic stem cells by cloning, or copying, cells.

Some stem cells come from adults. They may not live as long, and they may not develop into as many types of tissue as embryonic stem cells. They are also harder to gather.

Many people are opposed to the use of stem cells from embryos on ethical grounds. They do not think that it is right to use embryos in this way. They see embryos as living human beings. They do not like the fact that the embryos are destroyed in the process of gathering the stem cells.

However, others say that the embryos used for such research come from people who want to donate them for research. They see the embryos as collections of cells, and they think that the research is important because it could help improve the lives of many people.

ANATOMY AND MORPHOLOGY

Anatomists study the structure of organisms. Some morphological research compares homologous (similar in origin) or analogous (similar in function) structures among different species to establish relationships between them. Other studies may investigate the function or mode of operation of an anatomical feature. Histology (study of tissues) and

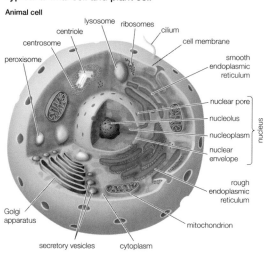

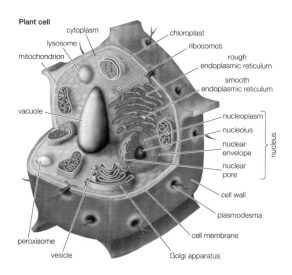

A plant cell (bottom) *features several structures that an animal cell* (top) *does not have, including chloroplasts, which facilitate photosynthesis.* Encyclopedia Britannica, Inc.

cytology (study of cells) are specialized areas of morphology.

PHYSIOLOGY

A physiologist studies the functions of organs and tissues. A cell physiologist investigates processes at the subcellular level. Animal or plant physiologists may study entire systems, such as those of circulation or respiration. Many physiological studies are intimately associated with morphology.

GENETICS AND MOLECULAR BIOLOGY

Molecular biology and genetics are two of the most dynamic fields of biology today. New laboratory techniques developed during the 20th century allowed scientists to examine the structure and function of biological molecules, such as DNA and proteins, and to determine their relationship to cellular structures, such as the nucleus and cell membrane. Geneticists also have benefited from molecular studies on genes and chromosomes. However, the use of genetic engineering in medicine and

agriculture has raised many new moral and philosophical issues.

ECOLOGY

Ecologists study the relationships and interactions between organisms and their environment by examining the structure and function of ecosystems. Many ecological studies require input from other scientific disciplines, such as geology,

Ecologists work to protect ecosystems such as Thailand's Khao Sok National Park, which is one of the oldest and most diverse rain forests in the world. Patryk Kosmider/Shutterstock.com

animal behavior, and botany. Policy makers and scientists interested in conservation issues need a solid understanding of ecology to understand how changes such as pollution and habitat destruction affect natural communities at both the local and the global level.

ETHOLOGY AND SOCIOBIOLOGY

Ethologists, or animal behaviorists, attempt to understand why animals behave the way they do. Some studies involve direct observations of animals in their native habitats, while others may involve experiments using laboratory animals. Ethology is tied closely to the fields of psychology and sociology. Sociobiology is concerned with the social interactions within a given species and focuses on such issues as whether certain traits, such as intelligence, are inherited or are culturally induced.

EVOLUTIONARY BIOLOGY

The evolution of species by natural selection is considered by the great majority of biologists to be a fundamental tenet of modern biology. Evolutionary biology seeks to answer questions about the origin and the genetic relationships of all living things. Some evolutionary biologists examine genetic relationships by comparing DNA sequences, while others may compare structural features or physiology. Many evolutionary biologists use knowledge gleaned from paleontology (the study of fossils).

Marine biologists track green sea turtles as they migrate hundreds of miles between their feeding sites and nesting sites. Gil Woolley-Scubazoo/Science Faction/Getty Images

OTHER AREAS OF STUDY

Although the previously named categories represent the major subdivisions of biology, there are many other research areas. Some are based on life in specific environments. Marine biology, for example, looks at many aspects of ocean life, whereas soil biology focuses on organisms and processes occurring in soil.

Many other scientific disciplines also require knowledge of biology. For example, biochemistry, a subdivision of organic chemistry, focuses on subcellular chemical processes and requires a solid foundation in cell biology.

CHAPTER 3

THE HISTORY OF BIOLOGY

No one knows precisely when humans first began to acquire knowledge of the natural world. Most experts believe that humans had been domesticating many animals and cultivating crops long before written records were kept. The earliest records show that the Assyrians and Babylonians had some knowledge of agriculture and medicine as early as 3500 BCE. By 2500 BCE this knowledge was widely applied by the major civilizations of China, Egypt, and India.

Opthalmology (the branch of medicine that deals with eye health) dates back to at least 1200 BCE in ancient Egypt. De Agostini Picture Library/Getty Images

THE GREEKS AND NATURAL LAW

The early Greeks were the first to formally investigate and describe the natural world. The concepts of cause and effect and that of a natural law that governs the universe were proposed around 600 BCE. Some 200 years later, the Greek physician Hippocrates observed among other things the effect of the environment on human nature.

In the mid-4th century BCE Aristotle presented the first system for classifying animals based on similarity of structure and function. His student Theophrastus drew up a scheme for classifying many of the plants. The writings of Galen, a Greek physician who lived in Rome during the 2nd century CE, influenced medicine for hundreds of years.

THE MIDDLE AGES

During the Middle Ages (roughly 500–1400 CE), the center of biological studies shifted from Europe to the Middle East. The Islamic scholar al-Jahiz expanded on the observations of the Greeks. His multivolume *Book of Animals* discussed a variety of topics, such as the relationships among different animal

Avicenna, also known as Ibn Sina, was an 11th-century Persian physician whose texts influenced medical study for centuries. Gianni Dagli Orti/The Art Archive at Art Resource, NY

groups and animal mimicry. The writings of the Persian physician Avicenna (Ibn Sina), based on the observations of Aristotle, helped revive European interest in biology.

A REBIRTH OF SCIENTIFIC LEARNING

Major biological advancements were made in Europe during the Renaissance (about 1300 to 1650 CE). The serious study of anatomy emerged in the 1500s through the efforts of Leonardo da Vinci and Andreas Vesalius, who documented the relationships between the anatomies of humans and of other animals. Advances in anatomy and physiology were made by means of dissection of organisms during the 16th and 17th centuries.

Prior to the 16th century, it was commonly believed that organisms such as flies and worms arose from mud or other inanimate matter. Although some scientists had previously disputed this idea of spontaneous generation, the concept remained untested. In 1668 the Italian physician Francesco Redi was the first to challenge the concept using a set of controlled experiments.

Interest in botany also increased during the 16th and 17th centuries. Numerous papers published by botanists such as Otto Brunfels of Germany and Gaspard Bauhin of Switzerland discussed horticulture and other plant-related topics.

FRANCESCO REDI

The 17th-century Italian physician Francesco Redi cast the first serious doubts on the theory of spontaneous generation. He demonstrated that maggots develop in rotting meat not spontaneously but rather from eggs laid on the meat by flies.

Redi was born on Feb. 19, 1626, in Arezzo, Italy. He read in a book on generation by physician William Harvey a speculation that vermin such as insects, worms, and frogs do not arise spontaneously, as was then commonly believed, but from seeds or eggs too small to be seen. In 1668, in one of the first examples of a biological experiment with proper controls, Redi set up a series of flasks containing different meats, half of the flasks sealed,

In addition to disproving spontaneous generation, Francesco Redi was among the first scientists to study parasites. age fotostock/SuperStock

half open. He then repeated the experiment but, instead of sealing the flasks, covered half of them with gauze so that air could enter. Although the meat in all of the flasks rotted, he found that only in the open and uncovered flasks, which flies had entered freely, did the meat contain maggots. Although he correctly concluded that the maggots came from eggs laid on the meat by flies, Redi, surprisingly, still believed that the process of spontaneous generation applied in such cases as gall flies and intestinal worms.

Redi is also known as a poet, chiefly for his *Bacco in Toscana* (1685; *Bacchus in Tuscany*). He died on Mar. 1, 1697, in Pisa, Italy.

DEVELOPMENT OF THE MICROSCOPE

The invention and development of the microscope in the 1600s generated an explosion of interest in biological studies. The value of this important new research tool was phenomenal. Unsuspected processes and organisms unknown to science were discovered in a flurry of biological investigation. Antonie van Leeuwenhoek reported his observations of single-celled animal-like creatures (protozoa) invisible to the naked eye. He subsequently observed spermatozoa, leading to new questions and interpretations of the male role in

Antonie van Leeuwenhoek's work in microbiology helped lay the foundations for the study of single-celled organisms, such as bacteria. NYPL/Science Source/Photo Researchers/ Getty Images

fertilization and reproduction. The concept of cells was introduced in 1665, when the English physicist Robert Hooke reported on the presence of tiny compartments in tissue he was studying under a microscope. Hooke named the compartments "cells." Marcello Malpighi used the microscope to observe and describe many microscopic structures, including red blood cells. Many other contributions to biology were made during this period as a result of discoveries in this previously unseen microscopic world.

CHAPTER 4

WHAT DEFINES A LIVING THING?

ells are the building blocks of the living world. Living things as diverse as bacteria, archaea, algae, fungi, protozoans, animals, and plants all consist of one or more cells. Cells are made up of components that help living things to eat, respire, excrete wastes, and perform all of the necessary functions of life. The components are organized, which means that they fit and work together. For this reason, living things are called organisms.

The activities of the cell are controlled by the cell's genetic material—its DNA. In some types of organisms, called eukaryotes, the DNA is contained within a membrane-bound structure called the nucleus. The term *eukaryote* derives from the Greek *eu* (true) and *karyon* (nucleus). In eukaryotic cells, most specialized tasks, such as obtaining energy from food molecules and producing material for cell growth, occur within a number of enclosed bodies called organelles. Many microorganisms, namely bacteria and archaea, consist of a single cell lacking this complex structure, and their DNA is not contained in a distinct nucleus. These organisms are called prokaryotes, from the Greek *pro* (before) and *karyon*.

Prokaryotic organisms are believed to have evolved before eukaryotes. Prokaryotic organisms such as the cyanobacteria can photosynthesize food; their food-making chlorophyll

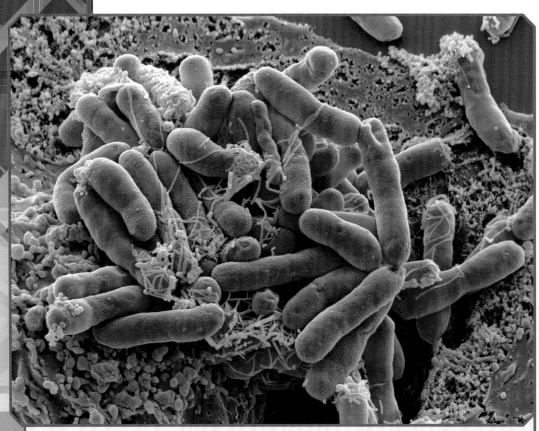

One of the best-known prokaryotic organisms is E. coli, *a bacterium that can cause food poisoning if consumed in contaminated water or transmitted through the bite of an insect.* Steve Gschmeissner/Science Photo Library/Getty Images

is scattered through the cell. In eukaryotic photosynthesizing organisms, such as plants and algae, the chlorophyll is contained within chloroplasts. Other types of bacteria do not have chlorophyll and are heterotrophic (they must obtain their food from other organisms).

Scientists once believed that prokaryotic organisms were the simplest organisms. Then viruses were discovered. A virus is a very small

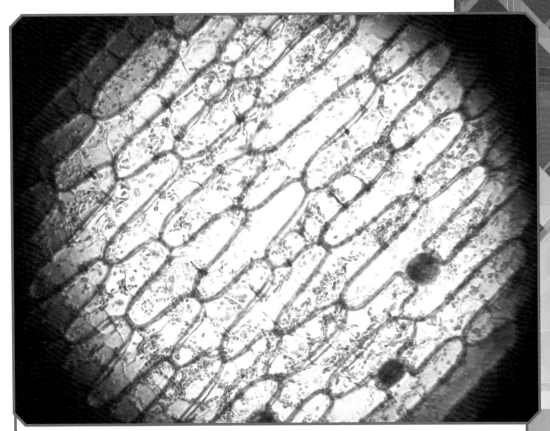

Chloroplasts, seen here under a microscope, are the cell parts that conduct photosynthesis. Dimarion/Shutterstock.com

infective particle composed of a nucleic acid core and a protein capsule. Viruses are responsible for many diseases of plants and animals, and some even infect bacteria and archaea. A virus is not a cell itself, but it requires a cell of a living organism to reproduce, or replicate. The nucleic acid inside the viral capsule carries the genetic information that is essential for replication of the virus. However, this is not enough for replication to take place—the virus requires the chemical building blocks and energy contained in living cells in order to reproduce. When a virus is not in a living cell it cannot replicate, though it may remain viable for some time. Scientists still do not agree that viruses are actually living things, since these entities cannot sustain life on their own.

LIFE IN A SINGLE-CELLED ORGANISM

There are many kinds of single-celled organisms that are not prokaryotes. Some of these single-celled eukaryotes look like slippers, vases, or balls, and some even have more than one nucleus. Many swim by waving a flagellum, a lashlike structure. Others use hairlike structures, which are called cilia. One kind has a mouth and a ring of moving "hairs" that bring

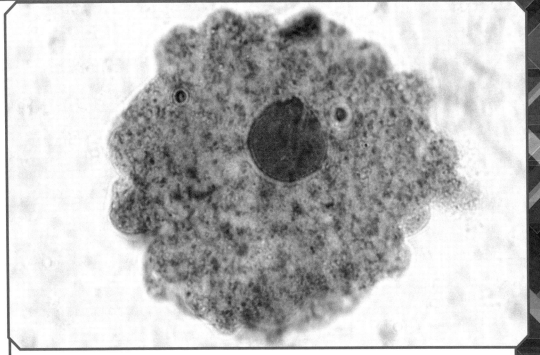

An amoeba moves by forming temporary cytoplasmic extensions called pseudopodia ("false feet"). This is considered to be the most primitive form of animal locomotion. Datacraft Co Ltd/ Getty Images

in food. It also has a stalk that can stretch or coil up and pull the cell away from danger.

A well-known example of a single-celled eukaryote is the amoeba, a protozoan that lives in freshwater ponds. To the unaided eye it looks like a milky speck, but a microscope shows that the protozoan's "body" is composed largely of a jellylike substance called cytoplasm that contains a nucleus and a number of specialized structures called organelles. The surface of the amoeba's cell is a clear, tough membrane that covers and protects the cytoplasm of the cell. The cell membrane is flexible and permits the amoeba to change shape as the cytoplasm flows within the cell. By doing so the amoeba can move to get food. It takes in a particle of food by surrounding it and enclosing it within a droplet called a vacuole. As it absorbs food, it grows. In due time it divides, and each half takes its share of the cytoplasm. The two halves of the amoeba become two new amoebas.

Another example of life in a single eukaryotic cell may be seen in the tiny green algae

Algae contribute to the productivity and health of ponds, but too much will overtake other organisms. Nagel Photography/Shutterstock.com

known as *Protococcus*. Layers of these algae can form green scum on damp trees, rocks, and brick walls. Like the amoeba, each *Protococcus* cell contains cytoplasm and a nucleus, as well as numerous organelles. The cell is covered with a membrane. The nucleus controls the life of the cell and in time divides for reproduction. Inside the cell is a chloroplast, a relatively large organelle filled with grains of chlorophyll. Using the energy of sunlight, these grains make food for the alga from water and carbon dioxide. Since the alga can make food in this way, it does not have to move about like an amoeba. Therefore it can have a stiff, protecting wall, made of a transparent layer of cellulose. These two substances, chlorophyll and cellulose, are also found in plants.

MULTICELLULAR ORGANISMS

Plants and animals are much larger than viruses and microorganisms. They also are too big to be formed by a single cell. They therefore are made of many cells that live and work together.

Some of the simplest multicellular organisms are certain algae that live in ponds and streams. Each alga consists of a chain of cells

that drifts about in the water. Most cells in the chain are alike, but the one at the bottom, called a holdfast, is different. It is long and tough. Its base holds to rocks or pieces of wood to keep the alga from floating away.

Sea lettuce, another type of multicellular algae, also has a holdfast. The rest of the plant contains boxlike cells arranged in two layers. These layers are covered and protected by two sheets of clear cellulose that is very tough.

Trees, weeds, and most other familiar land plants contain many more cells than sea lettuce and are much more complex. Their cells form organs such as roots, stems, leaves, and flowers. Millions of individual cells are needed to form these complex plants.

No animal consists simply of cells arranged in two flat layers like the sea lettuce. But the body of a pond-dwelling animal called *Hydra* has just two layers of cells arranged in a tube. The bottom of the tube is closed, but its top contains a mouth. Slender branches of the tube form tentacles that catch food and put it into the mouth.

Great numbers of cells of many kinds form the bodies of such creatures as insects, fish, and mammals. Similar cells that work together make up tissues. Tissues that work together form organs. A dog's heart, for example, is an organ composed of muscle tissue, nerve tissue, connective tissue, and covering tissue. Another kind of tissue, the blood, nourishes them. All these tissues work together when the dog's heart contracts.

THE PARTS OF COMPLEX ORGANISMS ARE CONTROLLED

The parts of a multicellular organism are controlled so that they work together. In plants, control is carried out by chemical substances called hormones. They go directly from cell to cell or are carried about in sap. When something touches a sensitive plant, for instance, the touched cells produce a hormone that goes to countless other cells and makes them lose water and collapse. As cell after cell does this, leaves begin to droop. They will not spread out again until the effect of the hormones is lost.

In multicellular animals, hormones regulate growth, keep muscles in condition, and perform many similar tasks. Other controls are carried out by nerve cells via impulses to and from various parts of the body. These impulses can indicate that something has been seen, felt, or heard. They also make muscle cells contract or relax, so that animals can

run, lie down, catch food, and do countless other things. Nerve cells may even deliver the impulses that stimulate hormone production.

LIVING THINGS ARE SPECIALIZED

Single-celled organisms can have specialized parts, such as flagella or cilia, which are used in swimming as well as in setting up currents that bring food. The food is swallowed through a mouthlike structure and digested in droplets called vacuoles that circulate through the cellular cytoplasm. Special fibers that work like nerves control the cilia and flagella. Several unicellular organisms even possess specialized photoreceptors, sometimes called eyespots, that respond to light.

These structures are said to be specialized because each one does its own part in the work of living. Multicellular organisms have tissues and organs that are still more specialized. Roots, leaves, flowers, eyes, and brains are examples of organs that do specialized work.

Specialization is carried from parts to entire living things. Cactus plants, for example, can live well only in dry regions, but cattails must grow in wet places. Herring swim near the surface of the sea, but the deep-sea angler fish lives on the bottom. Certain caterpillars eat only one kind of leaf.

This specialization of whole organisms is called adaptation. Every living thing is adapted to its surroundings—to the sea, freshwater, land, or even to living in or on other organisms. During the 3.5 billion years since living things evolved on Earth, organisms have become adapted to all sorts of conditions through the process known as evolution by natural selection. Today there are millions of different combinations between organisms and surroundings.

NATURAL SELECTION AND ADAPTATION

The process by which a species becomes better suited to its environment is called adaptation. It occurs when natural selection acts on a heritable trait, or characteristic, that allows an individual to better survive in its environment. Organisms with such a trait are more likely to thrive and reproduce in that environment and pass the beneficial trait on to their offspring. In contrast, individuals in the same environment that lack the adaptive trait are less likely to survive and produce offspring. Over time, more members of the population will have the adaptive trait relative to those that lack it.

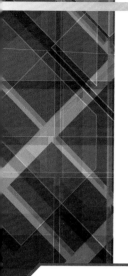

ATOMS IN LIVING MOLECULES

When atoms, the basic units of chemical elements, combine into chemical compounds, they form molecules. Proteins and other types of molecules found in cells can be extremely complex. One such protein, called

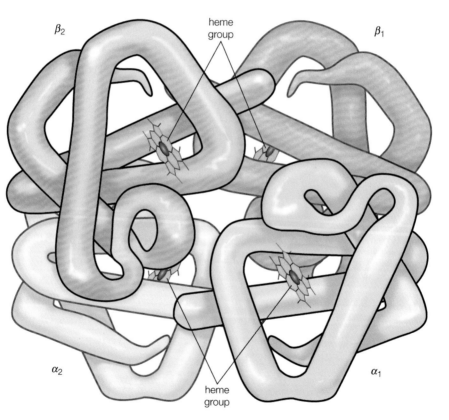

Hemoglobin is a protein made up of four polypeptide chains (a_1, a_2, β_1, and β_2), each attached to a heme group (an organic ringlike compound attached to an iron atom). © 2007 Encyclopædia Britannica, Inc.

hemoglobin, carries oxygen in the blood and is what makes blood red. Hemoglobin contains atoms of six different elements—carbon, hydrogen, oxygen, nitrogen, sulfur, and iron.

The complexity is made possible by carbon, which may be called the framework element. Because of its structure, carbon can link different kinds of atoms in various proportions and arrangements. Carbon atoms also join with each other in long chains and other arrays to make some of the most complex compounds known to chemistry.

Three other commonly found elements, oxygen, hydrogen, and nitrogen, are also important in the structure and function of living things. In the human body, for example, these elements, together with carbon, make up about 96 percent of the body's weight. Oxygen and hydrogen are highly important in body processes that obtain and use energy from food. Water, a compound of oxygen and hydrogen, plays a very important role in life processes. Large amounts of nitrogen are found in protein, or body-building compounds. Nitrogen also is found in wood and in the substance called chitin that forms the shells of crustaceans, insects, jointed worms, and related creatures.

HOW ALGAE AND PLANTS OBTAIN FOOD

As we have learned, all living things get food in one of two ways: they make it or they get it ready-made. The single-celled alga *Protococcus* uses both methods. It uses photosynthesis to manufacture food from water and carbon dioxide. The process requires energy, which it obtains from sunlight. After several steps the food-making process results in a kind of sugar called glucose. This sugar is the fundamental nutrient required by all living cells for energy.

Protococcus may use glucose molecules almost as fast as it makes them. It also may turn them into starch or droplets of oil, which it stores for use when it cannot get sunlight. Finally, *Protococcus* may combine atoms from glucose with some ready-made food combinations in the dissolved minerals. In this way it builds up protoplasm and cellulose.

Plants also make glucose via photosynthesis. In doing so, however, they use many different cells, tissues, and organs, such as leaves, roots, and sap-carrying channels in the stem.

HOW ANIMALS OBTAIN FOOD

Although many animals are green, animals do not contain chlorophyll. Therefore they cannot make food from carbon dioxide and water. This means that animals must get their food from other organisms, such as plants or other animals.

Like plants and algae, animals use food to produce different kinds of substances after they eat it. Animals use these substances for energy. They can turn sugary food into a starch called glycogen and store it in the liver, where it is ready for use when needed. When they eat more food than they need, they can store the extra food as fat.

SECURING ENERGY FROM FOOD

When plants make glucose from water and carbon dioxide, some atoms of oxygen are released from the combined materials. More oxygen is lost when glucose is converted into common sugar, starch, fat, or other food substances. As oxygen is removed, energy is stored in the made-over molecules.

The stored energy can later be obtained by cells through what is essentially a reverse process called oxidation. In a complex series of steps, oxygen is combined with food molecules, which change into simpler substances and give up energy. If complete oxidation takes place, the food becomes water and carbon dioxide again and gives up all its stored energy. Part of this energy is lost, but most of it remains available to the cell to carry out the functions of living.

Some organisms, especially microorganisms, can live in environments with little to no oxygen. These organisms also secure energy through chemical processes that change foods into simpler compounds. In one such process, called alcoholic fermentation, food gives up stored energy and changes into ethanol (a form of alcohol) and carbon dioxide. Alcoholic fermentation by yeast organisms in bread dough, for example, changes sugar into alcohol and carbon dioxide. The carbon dioxide is what makes the dough rise, and the alcohol evaporates as the bread is baked.

CARRYING FOOD AND OXYGEN

Single-celled organisms such as *Protococcus* get food-making substances and energy through their cell wall. In multicellular plants each cell also exchanges substances through its wall. To provide what every cell needs and to carry off wastes the plant uses a liquid called sap, which travels through specialized cells in the plant. The larger multicellular animals provide for the needs of their cells with circulating liquids called blood and lymph. Blood carries the oxygen needed to release energy from food, and it carries away the carbon dioxide and water produced as wastes by cellular processes. Lymph is a fluid that circulates through its own system in the body, playing an important role in the immune system as well as helping the blood dispose of wastes from tissues.

CHAPTER 5

TYPES OF LIVING THINGS

Some scientists estimate that there are roughly 14 million species on Earth, though only approximately 1.9 million have been identified. For centuries scientists divided living things into two kingdoms—plants and animals. Most organisms classified in the plant kingdom had chlorophyll and cellulose. The animal kingdom consisted of species that lacked chlorophyll or cellulose. This classification system was formalized in the 18th century by the biologist Carolus Linnaeus.

The system of Linnaeus was based on similarities in body structure, and it was completed more than a hundred years before the work of Charles Darwin, whose theory of evolution showed that the similarities

Carolus Linnaeus developed the first classification of living things. His system of naming organisms by their genus and species is still used today. Leemage/Universal Images Group/Getty Images

and differences of organisms could be viewed as a product of evolution by natural selection. As biologists in the 20th century learned more about microorganisms and fungi, they recognized the need for a different classification system that would draw on the evolutionary relationships among organisms. A five-kingdom system began to be adopted in the 1970s that separated fungi into their own kingdom. It also created a kingdom called Monera for all prokaryotes and a kingdom called Protista for all eukaryotes that did not belong in the plant, animal, or fungi kingdoms.

In the late 1970s, however, a group of scientists determined the existence of a previously unknown form of life. Using molecular technology to examine the evolutionary relationship among several groups of prokaryotes, the researchers noted that one group had distinct differences in its genetic code that set it apart from other prokaryotes. These findings eventually led to a significant modification in the classification of living things because these organisms, now called archaea, became recognized by most biologists as one of three distinct branches of life that formed early in the development of life on Earth. The three branches, called domains, are the Archaea, Bacteria, and Eukarya. The domain Eukarya encompasses all eukaryotes, namely protists, fungi, plants, and animals.

BACTERIA

Bacteria are single-celled prokaryotes (organisms with no distinct nuclei or organelles). Virtually all bacteria have a rigid cell wall, which contains a substance called peptidoglycan. Typical shapes of bacteria cells include spheres, rods, and spirals. Some bacteria have flagella that they use to propel themselves. Based on genetic studies experts believe there

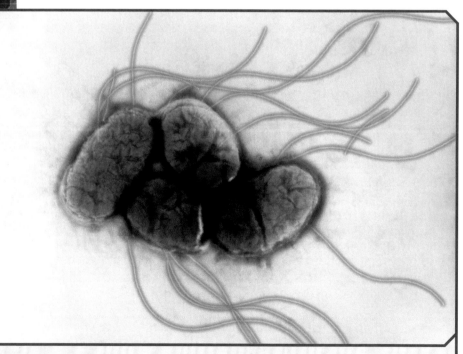

The long tails extending from this Serratia *bacterium are flagella that allow the cell to move.*
Kwangshin Kim/Photo Researchers/Getty Images

may be approximately 1 million species of bacteria of which only roughly 4,000 have been identified.

As a group, bacteria are highly diverse. Some bacteria are aerobic, and others are anaerobic. Some, such as purple bacteria and cyanobacteria, contain chlorophyll and therefore can make their own food. Purple bacteria swim by means of flagella. Although they are photosynthetic, the greenish particles they contain are a different form of chlorophyll than that found in other photosynthetic organisms. Cyanobacteria have no flagella and often live together in chains or clumps covered by a jellylike substance. They contain true chlorophyll and thus are autotrophic (they can produce their own food). However, under certain conditions they may also take in food from other sources. Most bacteria are heterotrophic, including an important group of bacteria that decompose the matter from dead organisms. Other important groups of bacteria include disease-causing bacteria and bacteria that convert nitrogen in the air into compounds that plants can use.

ARCHAEA

Archaea, like bacteria, are single-celled prokaryotes, and their external appearance is

similar to that of bacteria. Nevertheless, they differ from bacteria genetically and in terms of structural components and biochemistry. For example, the cell wall of archaea does not contain peptidoglycan, and the way archaea process DNA is more complex. Although abundant numbers of archaea live in a great variety of habitats, including in the oceans and in soil, a notable characteristic of certain species is that they can thrive in environments that are deadly to other kinds of organisms.

Methane, or marsh gas, is prevalent in swamps and marshes because it is a by-product of methanogens under the surface. Stephen Saks/Lonely Planet Images/Getty Images

Many archaea inhabit the deep vents on the ocean floor or hot springs, where temperatures are well over 200 °F (93 °C). *Pyrococcus woesei* is a notable example. It grows at temperatures above 212 °F (100 °C). Other such extremophile species of archaea live in pools of highly acidic or salty water. Archaea known as methanogens live in environments such as swamp mud or in the rumens of cows, where there is no oxygen. They take in carbon dioxide and hydrogen from their environment and produce methane gas as a by-product of their metabolism.

In a sense, these habitats resemble some of the early conditions on Earth, such as boiling hot water springs and an atmosphere devoid of oxygen. The ability of archaea to thrive in such extreme conditions suggests that they had become adapted to them long ago, and the pattern of the genetic code of archaea has suggested that these organisms were probably among the earliest forms of life on Earth. In other comparisons with bacteria, some archaea, like certain bacteria, are able to make nitrogen in the atmosphere available to plants. Unlike bacteria, no species of archaea has been found that uses chlorophyll for photosynthesis, and no archaea that cause disease in humans have been identified.

Archaea are difficult to identify and study because most cannot be grown in a laboratory culture. Advances in DNA techniques, however, make it possible to analyze directly material from the environment to identify the DNA and RNA of the archaea and other microorganisms inhabiting the sample.

PROTISTS

Protists are a very diverse group of mostly single-celled organisms that are eukaryotes—that is, they have a true nucleus and organelles—and are not considered to belong to the animal, plant, or fungi kingdoms. They may live as solitary individuals or in groups called colonies, and they may be autotrophic or heterotrophic. Under the five-kingdom classification, protists made up the kingdom Protista, and under the three-domain system most biologists continued to use that classification. Advances in comparing the genetic information from many kinds of protists indicated, however, that new kingdoms might be needed for their classification, and researchers sought to characterize them. It is estimated that there are some 600,000 species of protists on Earth, but only a fraction of these—roughly 80,000—have been described.

Many protists live in the oceans or in fresh-water. The protists are commonly divided into the animal-like protozoa, most of which are heterotrophic; the plantlike algae, which are autotrophic; and the funguslike slime molds and water molds, which are sapropha-gous. Among the better-studied protists are euglenoids, paramecia, and diatoms. Some protozoa have flagella or cilia to help propel them through their environment. This helps them to capture food and evade predators. Protozoa such as the euglenoids have chloro-phyll and can make glucose via photosynthesis, though they may also capture food from out-side sources under certain conditions. Green algae, as discussed earlier, also are autotrophic and manufacture food via photosynthesis. A number of protists cause important diseases. The flagellate protist *Trypanosoma* causes the disease African sleeping sickness in humans, while a particular species of amoeba is respon-sible for a form of dysentery.

FUNGI

The fungi kingdom contains a widely diverse group of organisms, ranging from yeasts to molds and mildews to mushrooms and toadstools. A fungus is categorized as a heterotrophic eukaryotic organism with cell walls. In addition, all fungi are multicellular. The presence of cell walls in these organisms inspired biologists to classify them for many years with the plants. However, fungi possess many traits not found in plants. Fungi lack chlorophyll and chloroplasts; they cannot synthesize their own food but rather must depend on other organisms for nourishment. Many fungi do this via symbiotic relationships with other organisms. Like animals, fungi must digest their food before absorbing it, but unlike animals, fungi digest their food outside of their bodies. To do this, fungi secrete enzymes into their immediate surroundings; these enzymes degrade, or break

SYMBIOSIS

A close living arrangement between two different species is called symbiosis. The word comes from the Greek word meaning "state of living together." Usually the two organisms are in close physical contact, with one living on or in the other. Symbiosis is classified as mutualism (once called simply symbiosis), which is mutually beneficial; commensualism, which is beneficial to one but neither harmful or beneficial to the other; or parasitism, which is beneficial to one and harmful to the other organism.

down, food into small molecules that are then absorbed by the fungi. According to scientific estimates, there are roughly 1.5 million species of fungi on Earth, though only 80,000 are known.

PLANTS

The plants are multicellular eukaryotic organisms and are classified in the kingdom Plantae. Members of the plant kingdom range from simple green vines and moss to enormous complex trees such as redwoods. Biologists believe there are approximately 300,000 species of plants. Of these, an estimated 10 percent have not been identified, and experts believe most of these exist in rain forests.

Virtually all plants contain chlorophyll and are autotrophs. Some plants are vascular—that is, they have specialized tissues that carry water and nutrients to all parts of the plant. Vascular plants include the flowering plants, the trees, and most familiar terrestrial plants. Other plants are nonvascular; they lack roots, stems, and leaves and are usually aquatic. Some terrestrial plants, including mosses and liverworts, also are nonvascular. Terrestrial nonvascular plants are usually small. Their lack of a vascular system limits the amount of nutrients that can

be transported to all of their cells. A few species of plants such as dodder and Indian pipe are nonphotosynthetic parasites, and a few others such as the Venus's-flytrap are photosynthetic but carnivorous—they trap insects as a source of nitrogen and minerals.

ANIMALS

The organisms classified in the kingdom Animalia are multicellular eukaryotes. Because their cells lack chlorophyll, all animals are heterotrophs. They have different types of tissues in their bodies and usually can move freely. Animals are sometimes called metazoans, which thus distinguishes them from the protozoans, which are single-celled.

Animals can be divided into two main groups: invertebrates and vertebrates. The invertebrates—such as insects, sea stars (starfish), and worms—lack a backbone. The body tissues of many invertebrates are supported by some type of outer structure, called an exoskeleton. Vertebrates have a backbone. Animals categorized as vertebrates include fish; amphibians, such as frogs and salamanders; reptiles, such as snakes and lizards; birds; and mammals, such as dogs, cows, horses, monkeys, and humans.

Sea stars are often called starfish, but unlike fish, they do not have a backbone and are thus classified as invertebrate animals. Paul Kennedy/Lonely Planet Images/Getty Images

The animal kingdom is by far the largest kingdom of eukaryotes. Experts believe that there are more than 10 million species of animals living today; of these, only about 1.3 million species have been identified. The largest group within the animal kingdom is the insects. Roughly 8 million species of insects may exist, but only about one million have been identified or described. The best known of the animal groups are birds and mammals, of which roughly 10,000 and 4,500 species have been identified, respectively.

CHAPTER 6

THE EVOLUTION OF LIVING THINGS

L iving things include many kinds of organisms, from the plants, animals, fungi, and algae that can be readily seen in nature, to the multitude of tiny creatures known as protozoa, bacteria, and archaea that can be seen only with a microscope. Living things can be found in every type of habitat on Earth—on land and in lakes, rivers, and oceans. Although all these organisms are very different from one another, they all have two things in common: they are all descended from a single ancient ancestor, and they are all alive.

Most scientists believe that the first living organism on Earth probably evolved within a billion years of Earth's formation, which occurred roughly 4.5 billion years ago. This belief is based on evidence from the fossil record. Fossil remains of microorganisms resembling cyanobacteria (a group of microorganisms formerly known as blue-green algae) were discovered embedded in rocks that were roughly 3.5 billion years old.

Scientists can learn about organisms that lived millions of years ago from their fossils, such as these found at the Middle Jurassic Carmel Formation in Utah. Mark A. Wilson (Department of Geology, The College of Wooster)

The early Earth was very different from the Earth of today. The atmosphere was rich in hydrogen, which was critical to the chemical cvents that later took place. According to one scientific hypothesis, soupy mixtures of elements important to life, such as carbon, nitrogen, oxygen, and hydrogen, were concentrated in warm pools bathed in the ultraviolet rays of the sun. Out of this mix, chemical elements combined in reactions that grew increasingly

complex, forming organic molecules such as proteins and nucleic acids. As they combined and recombined, these molecules eventually formed a highly primitive cell capable of reproducing itself. Over millions of years, the process of natural selection then aided the evolution of single-celled and multicelled organisms from an ancient common ancestor.

SEVEN FUNCTIONS OF LIVING THINGS

There are seven key functions, or processes, necessary for life. To be categorized as a living thing, an organism must be able to do all of these.

MOVEMENT

Living things have the ability to move in some way without outside help. The movement may consist of the flow of material within the organism or external movement of the organism or parts of the organism.

SENSITIVITY

Living things respond to conditions around them. For example, green plants grow toward

All plants, such as the sunflowers shown here, need light to conduct photosynthesis. liseykina/ Shutterstock.com

sunshine, certain microorganisms shrink into tiny balls when something touches them, and human beings blink when light shines into their eyes.

RESPIRATION

All living organisms must be capable of releasing energy stored in food molecules through a chemical process known as cellular

respiration. In aerobic respiration, oxygen is taken up and carbon dioxide is given off. In single-celled organisms, the exchange of these gases with the environment occurs across the organism's cellular membrane. In multicellular organisms, the exchange of the gases with the environment is slightly more complex and usually involves some type of organ specially adapted for this purpose. Large multicellular animals such as birds and mammals must breathe in oxygen, which travels to the lungs and is transferred to the blood flow of the body's arteries. The arterial system carries this fresh oxygen to all the tissues and cells of the body, where it is exchanged for carbon dioxide, a cellular waste product that must be carried back to the lungs so that the organism can exhale it. Plants respire, too, but they do it through openings called stomata, which are found on the underside of their leaves. Certain types of bacteria and archaea use a type of cellular respiration, called anaerobic respiration, in which the role of oxygen is carried out by other reactants. Anaerobic respiration may make use of carbon dioxide or nitrate, nitrite, or sulfate ions, and it allows the organism to live in an environment without oxygen.

NUTRITION

Living things require energy in order to survive. The energy is derived from nutrients, or food. Green plants, algae, and certain archaea and bacteria can make food from water and carbon dioxide via photosynthesis. Plants called legumes can make proteins by taking up nitrogen provided by bacteria that live in nodules in the plant's roots. Animals, fungi, protozoa, and many archaea and bacteria need to get food from an outside source. They do this in different ways, all of which depend on what physical adaptations the organism has.

Carnivorous plants such as the tropical pitcher plant derive nutrients from trapping and consuming insects or other animals. Bahadir Yeniceri/ Shutterstock.com

Some animals such as mammals bite into their food with teeth; certain insects suck up nectar from flowers. Many species of protozoa and bacteria take in nutrients through membranes that cover their bodies.

Regardless of how nutrients are obtained—or, in the case of autotrophic organisms, manufactured—the organism's physical state will determine how the nutrients are used. Some of the nutrients may be used for structural repairs—that is, turned into living material, such as bones, teeth, scales, or wood. Some portion of nutrients may be used to provide energy, which the organism needs in order to function. This can be compared to the process in which an engine burns oil or coal and gets energy to move a train. But note that an engine does not use coal or oil to make itself larger or mend parts, as living things do with food.

GROWTH

Snowballs will grow in size when they are rolled through snow, and salt crystals will grow in salty water as it evaporates. Although these lifeless objects become larger, they do not grow in the way that living things do. Living things grow by making new parts and materials and changing old ones. This happens when a seed grows into a plant or a chick matures into a hen. As human beings grow, they add new structures, such as teeth, and change the proportions of others.

A special kind of growth heals injuries. Shrubs and trees mend injuries by covering them with bark and adding new layers of wood. Crabs grow new legs when old ones are lost. Human beings can heal cut skin and mend broken bones.

REPRODUCTION

When living things reproduce, they make new living things. This is true even of the simplest microorganisms, which may reproduce by simply dividing into two parts. Each new part is able to move, feed, grow, and perform the other functions of living. This type of reproduction is called asexual because it can be performed without a mating partner. There are other forms of asexual reproduction, in addition to sexual reproduction, which requires a partner. Asexual reproduction is most commonly found among the so-called lower organisms, such as bacteria and some types of protozoa and fungi. They are called "lower" not because they are unimportant or

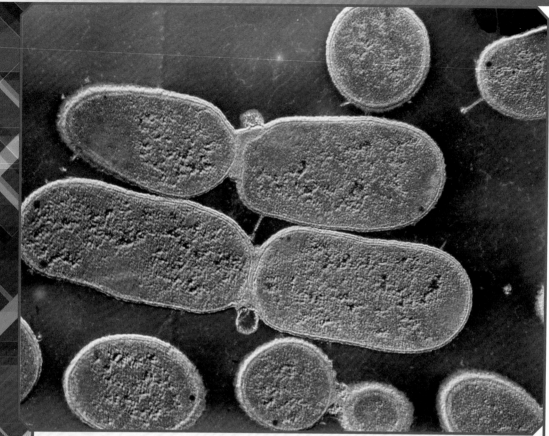

Bacteria reproduce through binary fission, a process in which the cell divides in half and becomes two separate organisms. CNRI/Science Source

simple, but rather because they evolved earlier than the complex "higher" organisms, such as vertebrates. Mammals and birds, for example, require a partner in order to reproduce. Some higher organisms, however, are able to reproduce asexually; certain plants are an example of this, as are some reptiles.

EXCRETION

All living organisms create waste products via the processes of living. Much waste comes from food. The rest is produced by movement, growth, and other functions of living. If this waste remained in living things, it would soon cause illness and death. Thus living things must have a way to dispose of waste matter. The process that removes waste products from the body is called excretion.

CHAPTER 7

TAXONOMY AND GENETICS

Naming organisms and establishing their relationships to one another comprise the field of taxonomy (also called systematics). Modern taxonomy is based on a system established in the 1750s by Swedish botanist Carolus Linnaeus.

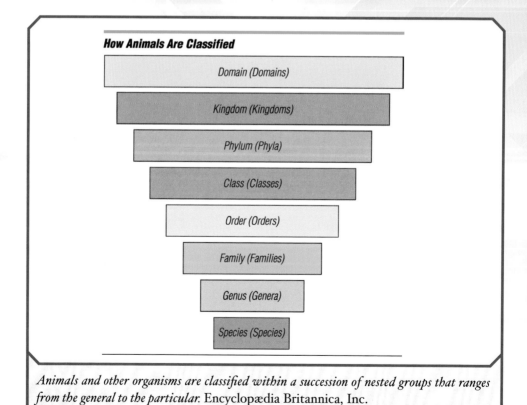

How Animals Are Classified

Domain (Domains)

Kingdom (Kingdoms)

Phylum (Phyla)

Class (Classes)

Order (Orders)

Family (Families)

Genus (Genera)

Species (Species)

Animals and other organisms are classified within a succession of nested groups that ranges from the general to the particular. Encyclopædia Britannica, Inc.

CAROLUS LINNAEUS

The Swedish naturalist and physician Carolus Linnaeus brought into general use the scientific system of classifying plants and animals that is now universally used. This is the binomial (two-name) system, in which each living thing is assigned a name consisting of two Latin words. The first word is the name of the genus and the second the species. So important was Linnaeus that he is called the Father of Systematic Botany.

Linnaeus was born Carl von Linné on May 23, 1707, in Rashult. (In later years he preferred the latinized form of his name.) Although his father, a curate, wanted the boy to follow in his footsteps, Carl was interested in plants and animals. He was nicknamed "the little botanist" when he was eight years old. The village physician saw that the boy had unusual gifts and encouraged the father to help care for Carl while he studied medicine at the University of Uppsala beginning in 1728.

There his talents soon won him an appointment as lecturer in botany. Later the Academy of Sciences of Uppsala sent him on a 5,000-mile (8,000-kilometer) botanical survey of Lapland. The scientific results of his journey were published in *Flora Lapponica* in 1737. His future wife, Sara Moraea, helped provide the funds with which he obtained his doctor's degree in medicine at a university in Holland.

In Holland Linnaeus became medical attendant to an Amsterdam banker who had a large botanical garden. Linnaeus was made director of this garden. In the next few years he published *Systema Naturae* (System of Nature) and *Genera Plantarum* (Genera of Plants). Into later editions of these he introduced his famous system of classification.

(continued on the next page)

After scientific journeys to France and England Linnaeus returned to Stockholm to practice medicine. In 1742 he was appointed to the chair of botany at Uppsala, where he spent the rest of his active life. Students came to him from many countries and searched the planet for specimens to contribute to his studies. Linnaeus died on Jan. 10, 1778, in Uppsala.

Linnaeus's system of classification was an artificial one. He himself regarded it as a temporary convenience to be replaced by a natural system whenever the fundamental relationships of plants became known. In the 19th century the theory of evolution supplied some of the principles needed for a natural system, but the broad outlines of Linnaeus's system were retained.

The Linnaean system classifies organisms based on shared attributes and the closeness of their evolutionary relationships. The most basic category is the species (spelled identically for both singular and plural forms). Individual members of a species share common characteristics and a closer genetic relationship with each other than they share with members of other species. The next highest taxon (level of organization) is the genus (plural, genera), which includes groups of related species.

All species have a two-part scientific name. The first part is the genus, or generic, name.

For example, wolves and coyotes belong to the same genus—*Canis*. The second part of the name is the specific name: wolves are members of the species *Canis lupus*, and coyotes belong to the species *Canis latrans*. The whole scientific name is always italicized; the generic name is capitalized, while the specific name is not.

The relatedness between groups within a taxon becomes increasingly distant at higher levels: genera with similar traits are grouped into the same "family"; related families are classified in the same "order"; related orders are placed into the same "class"; related classes are placed in the same "phylum"; related phyla (plural of phylum) are placed into a "kingdom"; and related kingdoms are placed into a "domain," the highest level of classification. The higher taxonomic levels indicate phylogenetic relationships—the degree to which species have diverged from each other during the course of evolution.

The classification of living things is frequently challenged and revised. Taxonomic studies may be based on morphological (structural) traits, such as skull shape and jaw length, or on molecular data, such as DNA, RNA, or protein sequences.

The publication in the 1750s of Carolus Linnaeus's biological classification scheme for organisms was a major advance in biology. Linnaeus was one of the first taxonomists to organize living things in a simple and logical manner, using a system of binomial nomenclature (two-part names) that appealed to most scientists. The Linnaean system indicates both the degree of similarity and difference among species, and it persists today as the basis for naming living things.

EVOLUTIONARY THEORY

New biological theories developed rapidly during the 18th and 19th centuries and challenged many old ideas. The British naturalist Charles Darwin published his theory about evolution in the book *On the Origin of Species by Means of Natural Selection* (1859). Darwin's ideas centered around observations he had made in the Galápagos Islands, an archipelago off the coast of Ecuador. Another British naturalist, Alfred Russel Wallace, made similar observations about animals in Indonesia, and the research of both scientists was presented simultaneously to their peers. Although Darwin's efforts received wider attention,

Charles Darwin began developing the theory of natural selection and evolution after observing wildlife on a five-year journey around the world on the HMS Beagle. Bob Thomas/Popperfoto/Getty Images

Wallace's observations about the geographic distribution of plants and animals remain vital in modern studies of evolution.

The concept of natural selection and evolution revolutionized 19th-century thinking about the relationships between groups of plants and animals and about speciation (the origin of new species). Darwin provided sound scientific reasoning for the wealth of biological variability and similarity that exists among living things. Although genetics and the mechanisms of inheritance were unknown during Darwin's time, he noted that certain life-forms were more likely to survive than others and proposed that this was influenced by variable traits (such as beak size in birds) that were passed from parents to offspring. This concept of natural selection provided the first scientific explanation of the variations observed in nature. Darwin also proposed that new species are formed—and others become extinct—by a gradual process of change and adaptation made possible by this natural variability. Although Darwin's ideas provoked tremendous controversy, they influenced biology more than any other concept and today are generally accepted by the scientific community.

MECHANISM OF HEREDITY

The mechanism that produced the heritable variation needed for natural selection was discovered in the mid-19th century by Gregor Mendel, an Austrian monk interested in plant breeding. Mendel's experiments with garden peas revealed that the peas inherited characteristics from their parents in a mathematically predictable fashion. His findings introduced the concept of the gene as the unit of inheritance, or heredity. Although Mendel published his results in 1866, the significance of his studies remained obscure until 1900. The rediscovery of Mendel's work and the discovery of chromosomes in the early 20th century spurred development of studies of genetics and heredity and strengthened science's understanding of evolution.

GREGOR MENDEL

The laws of heredity on which the modern science of genetics is based were discovered by an obscure Austrian monk named Gregor Mendel. His papers reached the largest libraries of Europe and the United States, yet Mendel's discoveries remained virtually unknown for more than 30 years after he completed his experiments.

(continued on the next page)

Johann Mendel was born on July 22, 1822, in Heinzendorf, Austria. He took the name Gregor when he entered the monastery in Brünn, Moravia (now Brno, Czech Republic) in 1843. He studied for two years at the Philosophical Institute in Olmütz (now Olomouc, Czech Republic), before going to Brünn. He became a priest in 1847. For most of the next 20 years he taught at a nearby high school, except for two years of study at the University of Vienna (1851–53). In 1868 Mendel was elected abbot of the monastery.

Gregor Mendel formulated the law of segregation (genes transfer as separate units) and the law of independent assortment (genes are inherited independently of genes on a different chromosome). Time & Life Pictures/Getty Images

Mendel's famous garden-pea experiments began in 1856 in the monastery garden. He proposed that the existence of characteristics such as blossom color is due to the occurrence of paired elementary units of heredity, now known as genes. Mendel presented his work to the local Natural Science Society in 1865 in a paper entitled "Experiments with Plant Hybrids." Administrative duties after 1868 kept him too busy for further research. He lived out his life in relative obscurity, dying on Jan. 6, 1884. In 1900, independent research by other scientists confirmed Mendel's results.

MODERN DEVELOPMENTS

During the 20th century, biology changed from a predominantly descriptive science to one keenly founded upon experimentation and deductive reasoning. Such discoveries as the use of antibiotics to treat infectious disease and insulin to treat diabetes, as well as increased knowledge about cell development, were among the many important advances made over the past 100 years or so.

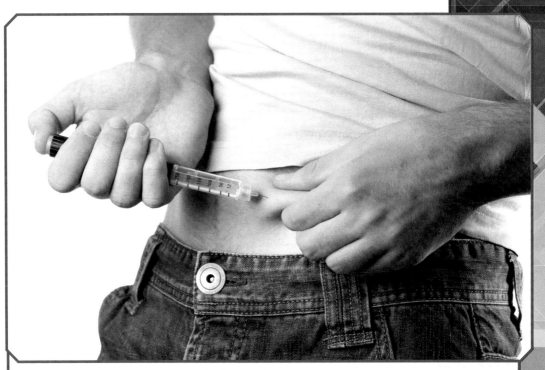

Individuals who have diabetes mellitus often get injections of insulin, a hormone of the pancreas, to correct the level of glucose in their blood. Alexander Raths/Shutterstock.com

A key turning point in biology was the discovery in 1953 of the structure of DNA and the subsequent unraveling of the genetic code of life. These discoveries aided science's understanding of genetic diseases in plants and animals and allowed for unprecedented discoveries in molecular biology. Advances in the technology for copying and manipulating DNA ushered in the age of biotechnology with practical applications in agriculture, industry, and medicine. It also enabled efforts to decipher the entire genetic code (genome) of many organisms. As genetic sequencing became faster and less expensive, it spurred biological research in such areas as the study of gene expression and function in biological processes.

Some developments had negative effects on the natural world, however. Increased urbanization and industrialization destroyed many habitats and threatened the existence of countless species, while pollution and the emergence of new infectious diseases such as AIDS endangered public health. The growth of biotechnology also raised concerns over its potential hazards to health and the environment and the need to monitor and regulate its use.

CONCLUSION

Just as life itself has evolved, so has the study of biology. Breakthrough technologies have given biologists the tools to investigate living things in greater depth. Important discoveries have provided new information and insight and sometimes debunked old beliefs. Biologists continue to discover new species of many kinds of organisms, and they estimate that, for example, some nine-tenths of the existing species of plants remain to be identified.

Categorizing life and understanding how life works and how it changes are among the fundamental challenges of biology. The field encompasses how the specific processes of life—such as respiration, nutrition, and reproduction—occur, as well as examining why those processes happen in the way that they do. As this knowledge is accumulated, it contributes to biology's larger questions, including how life-forms change, adapt to different environments, and relate to each other. With these answers, biologists can advance their understanding of how all organisms—large and small, simple and complex—play a part in the vast web of life on Earth.

GLOSSARY

aerobic Involving oxygen in a process.

autotrophic Self-nourishing; able to produce food from inorganic materials.

cellulose A stiff, tough substance found in the cell walls of plants to provide structure.

chlorophyll A green pigment found in plants that enables them to perform photosynthesis.

chromosome The part of a cell on which genes are carried.

cytoplasm The jellylike substance within a cell that contains the organelles and other living material of a cell, but not including the nucleus.

DNA The substance that carries genetic information.

enzyme A type of protein that is produced by cells and enables chemical processes.

extremophile An organism that lives in extreme environmental conditions.

heterotrophic Unable to produce food; obtaining organic material from outside sources.

membrane A thin, flexible sheet that surrounds the interior parts of a cell and protects them.

metabolism The chemical processes a plant or animal uses to convert food into energy.

mimicry The act of copying or imitating.

organ A part of the body, comprised of tissues, that performs a specific function.

organelle A part of a cell that performs a specific function.

photosynthesis A process in which plants convert light energy into food.

phylogenetic Involving similarities and differences between organisms based on natural evolutionary relationships.

protoplasm The liquid contents of a cell that include its living material, including the nucleus.

RNA The substance in cells that helps manufacture proteins.

saprophagous Feeding on decaying matter.

spontaneous generation The obsolete idea that life arises from inanimate matter.

symbiosis A relationship between organisms of two different species that live closely together.

tissue A group of cells that perform a specific function or form a specific part of a plant or animal.

American Institute of Biological Sciences
1900 Campus Commons Drive, Suite 200
Reston, VA 20191
(703) 674-2500
Website: http://www.aibs.org
AIBS is dedicated to promoting biological
   research and education to be used for the
   good of society. It works to disseminate
   information to biology professionals,
   government, and the public to help make
   informed decisions.

American Society for Cell Biology
8120 Woodmont Avenue, Suite 750
Bethesda, MD 20814-2762
(301) 347-9300
Website: http://www.ascb.org
ASCB is an international organization for
   scientists who study cells, the basic units
   of life. The society promotes scientific
   research and discovery, improvement in
   education, and sound research policies.

The American Society of Human Genetics
9650 Rockville Pike
Bethesda, MD 20814-3998

(301) 634-7300
Website: http://www.ashg.org
ASHG is a membership organization for genetics professionals. It works to promote and share research in the genetics community, and to further public education about genetic science and services.

American Society of Plant Biologists
15501 Monona Drive
Rockville, MD 20855-2768
(301) 251-0560
Website: http://my.aspb.org
Encouraging research and development in plant biology was the mission of the ASPB when it was founded in 1924. Since then it has expanded to include molecular and cellular biology among its areas of focus.

Association of Professional Biology
300-1095 McKenzie Avenue
Victoria, BC V8P 2L5
Canada
(250) 483-4283
Website: https://professionalbiology.com
An organization for professional biologists, the APB promotes using sound science in managing resources and making decisions, and

works to educate the public, government agencies, and other professions on the work of biologists.

National Science Foundation
4201 Wilson Boulevard
Arlington, VA 22230
(703) 292-5111
Website: http://www.nsf.gov
The NSF funds much of the basic science research in the United States. It monitors key areas of inquiry, chooses top scientists to conduct research, and ensures that the information is integrated with education.

WEBSITES

Because of the changing nature of Internet links, Rosen Publishing has developed an online list of websites related to the subject of this book. This site is updated regularly. Please use this link to access the list:

http://www.rosenlinks.com/SCI/Bio

FOR FURTHER READING

Abramovitz, Melissa. *Stem Cells*. Farmington Hills, MI: Lucent, 2012.

Allaby, Michael. *Ecology: Plants, Animals, and the Environment*. New York, NY: Facts On File, 2009.

Anderson, Michael, ed. *A Closer Look at Plant Reproduction, Growth, and Ecology*. New York, NY: Britannica Educational Publishing, 2011.

Boleyn-Fitzgerald, Miriam. *Biodiversity*. New York, NY: Facts On File, 2011.

Claybourne, Anna. *Complete Book of the Human Body*. London: Usborne Publishing Ltd., 2013.

Hollar, Sherman. *A Closer Look at Biology, Microbiology, and the Cell*. New York, NY: Britannica Educational Publishing, 2011.

Leone, Bruno. *Origin: The Story of Charles Darwin*. Greensboro, NC: Morgan Reynolds, 2009.

Mooney, Carla. *Genetics: Breaking the Code of Your DNA*. White River Junction, VT: Nomad Press, 2014.

Wanjie, Anne, ed. *The Basics of Biology*. New York, NY: Rosen Publishing, 2013.

INDEX

A

adaptation, 45, 80
aerobic respiration, 68
alcoholic fermentation, 50
algae, 40–42, 48, 49, 59
amoebas, 39–40, 41, 59
anaerobic respiration, 68
anatomy, 16, 21–23, 31
animals, 62–63
antibiotics, 83
arachnology, 15
archaea, 53, 55–58
Aristotle, 29, 31
atoms in living molecules,
    46–47
autotrophic organisms,
    55, 58, 59, 61, 70
Avicenna, 31

B

bacteria, 53, 54–55, 56, 57
Bauhin, Gaspard, 32
biochemistry, 15, 27
biology
    branches of, 18–27
    defined, 9, 12
    history of, 28–34
    modern developments,
      83–84
    subdivisions of, 14–17
bioluminescence, 14

biotechnology, 84
Book of Animals, 29–31
botany, 14, 31–32
Brunfels, Otto, 32
bryology, 15

C

carbon, 47, 65
carbon dioxide, 12, 41, 49,
    50, 51, 57, 68, 69
cell biology, 27
cells
    about, 35–36
    concept of, 34
cellular respiration, 67–68
cellulose, 41, 42, 48, 52
chlorophyll, 36–37, 41, 49,
    52, 55, 57, 59, 60, 61, 62
chloroplast, 41, 60
cloning, 18–19
commensualism, 60
cytology, 16, 23
cytoplasm, 39, 40, 41, 44

D

Darwin, Charles, 52–53,
    78–80
dissection, 31
DNA, 23, 26, 35, 36, 56,
    58, 77
    discovery of structure, 84